WOMEN IN WORLD WAR I

ESSENTIAL LIBRARY OF
WORLD WAR I

Essential Library

An Imprint of Abdo Publishing
abdopublishing.com

BY KRISTINE CARLSON ASSELIN

CONTENT CONSULTANT

JASON R. MYERS, PHD
INDEPENDENT SCHOLAR

abdopublishing.com

Published by Abdo Publishing, a division of ABDO, PO Box 398166, Minneapolis, Minnesota 55439. Copyright © 2016 by Abdo Consulting Group, Inc. International copyrights reserved in all countries. No part of this book may be reproduced in any form without written permission from the publisher. Essential Library™ is a trademark and logo of Abdo Publishing.

Printed in the United States of America, North Mankato, Minnesota

102015
012016

THIS BOOK CONTAINS
RECYCLED MATERIALS

Cover Photo: Paul Thompson/US Marine Corps History Division
Interior Photos: Paul Thompson/US Marine Corps History Division, 1; US Naval History and Heritage Command, 4, 11, 13, 99 (left); Miss G. H. Erd/US Naval History and Heritage Command, 7; Bain News Service/Library of Congress, 14, 17, 19, 35, 51, 59, 76, 98 (top); Everett Historical/Shutterstock Images, 23, 32, 42, 48, 61, 64, 68, 70, 83, 86; US Marine Corps History Division, 24, 28, 98 (bottom); Library of Congress, 29, 41, 47; Everett Collection/Newscom, 36, 73; Mondadori/Newscom, 54; Courtesy of the University of Illinois Archives, 56; Brown Brothers/National Geographic Creative/Corbis, 74; American National Red Cross/Library of Congress, 75; Bettmann/Corbis, 80, 89, 93, 99 (right); Wikimedia Commons, 81; Horace Nicholls/Imperial War Museum, 85; Igor Golovniov/Shutterstock Images, 91

Editor: Megan Anderson
Series Designers: Kelsey Oseid and Maggie Villaume

Library of Congress Control Number: 2015945640
Cataloging-in-Publication Data

Asselin, Kristine Carlson.
  Women in World War I / Kristine Carlson Asselin.
   p. cm. -- (Essential library of World War I)
  ISBN 978-1-62403-925-6 (lib. bdg.)
  Includes bibliographical references and index.
  1. World War, 1914-1918--Participation, Female--Juvenile literature. 2. World War, 1914-1918--War work--Women--Juvenile literature.   I. Title.
  940.3--dc23
                                                                                              2015945640

CONTENTS

For the first time, women were allowed to join the US Navy during World War I.

CHAPTER
1

IN THE NAVY

The United States was on the verge of entering World War I, and the US Navy was in trouble. An urgent shortage of staff meant every shore station needed clerical workers—people to help run the offices, such as stenographers and draftsmen. As more men were called up to military positions at sea, clerical positions sat vacant and work incomplete.

In the spring of 1917, US Secretary of the Navy Josephus Daniels mused to his advisers, "Is there any regulation yeoman *must* be a man?"[1] There was no rule specifically restricting women from enlisting in the navy as yeomen, or officers who serve as clerks. "Enroll women in the naval service as yeomen and we will have the best clerical assistance the country can provide," Daniels said.[2]

FIRST ENLISTEES

Loretta Perfectus Walsh was the first woman to answer the call. At age 18, Walsh enlisted in the navy on March 17, 1917, in Philadelphia, Pennsylvania. On April 6, 1917, the United States declared war on Germany. Walsh became the first woman to enlist in the US Navy and also the first woman to serve in the armed forces in a non-nurse position. Walsh was later promoted to chief petty officer—a rank responsible for training and supervising subordinates—during a four-year enlistment.

Another woman to enlist early on was Daisy Pratt Erd from Chicago, Illinois. Erd enlisted in Boston, Massachusetts, in April 1917. By May, she was promoted to chief yeoman and put in charge of all female employees at the Boston Navy Yard. Erd became responsible for accepting new recruits, but not all women who tried to join were approved. Erd said, "Most applicants can't spell. I give that

REQUIREMENTS

The requirements to enlist in the navy were not strict. Yeomen had to be between the ages of 18 and 35, in good health, and have a neat appearance. The navy preferred high school graduates, but yeomen did not need a college degree. After arriving at the recruitment station, a woman simply filled out the forms and had a quick physical exam to make sure she was in good health. Yeomanette Estelle Kemper described her physical: "Male recruits may not mind being herded together in the 'altogether,' but those poor stripped feminine patriots were a sorry sight, as they cringed in that open hallway, waiting to be scrutinized by a strange doctor in a navy uniform."[3] Recruits then took an oath and were sworn into the service for four years.

DAISY PRATT ERD
YEOMAN (F) AND SONGWRITER

Daisy Pratt Erd was not only one of the first women in the navy—she was also an accomplished songwriter. Erd wrote the music and lyrics to several patriotic songs, such as "We'll Carry the Star Spangled Banner Thru The Trenches," "Uncle Sam's Ships," and "Rear Admiral Wood One-Step." She donated the proceeds to the Naval Reserve Fund and the Navy Relief Society, charitable organizations that assisted navy veterans.

After two years in the navy, Erd organized 200 women into the first women's post of the American Legion in Boston. She also dedicated her time to instating a $100 Massachusetts state bonus for all women who had served in the navy and forming a union to secure jobs for women after the war ended. "The girls did a man's job, and why shouldn't we be treated like the men are treated in the matter of bonuses? We represent as fine a lot of young women as ever lived," Erd said.[4]

examination first. If the applicant fails to pass the spelling, I don't examine her further."[5] Despite this, Erd soon supervised more than 200 women.

These 200 women were the first officially recognized enlisted women in US military history. The navy didn't change the title for newly enlisted personnel, but some called these new recruits *yeomanettes*. The navy simply added an *F* for female in parentheses after the title.

Some of the jobs were boring, even though they were important to the navy's operations. Yeoman (F) Nell Weston Halstead asked her boss to give her more exciting work. Halstead said:

> *One day it got my goat so completely that I boldly sailed into the captain's office—he was an old-timer in the navy, with a basso voice and glowering eyes—and I told him we didn't like our jobs and we wanted to go to France.*[6]

Halstead was sternly instructed to return to her duties. Aside from the monotonous work, most yeomen (F) became accustomed to navy life and learned to obey orders without question. Women were not allowed to go to sea, but some were sent overseas to work with nurses in hospitals in France and bases outside the continental United States.

Most women enlisted in the US Navy worked six days a week for ten hours a day. The navy did not provide much training before sending yeomanettes to naval bases and offices all over the country, including Guam and Puerto Rico. But some jobs required more skills. Yeomanettes who had additional skills were also permitted to fill noncombatant, or nonfighting, jobs. Among those were stenographers, electricians, pharmacists, chemists, and telephone operators.

Many had very little education and took night classes to gain clerical skills necessary for their new jobs. They learned naval terms, regulations, and procedures. They weren't expected to carry weapons, but practiced marching and simple formations for 30 minutes once a week.

One yeoman (F), teacher Lou MacPherson Guthrie, worked the graveyard shift, midnight to 8 a.m., in the Navy Yard for the Bureau of War Risk and Insurance. Guthrie remembered,

> We liked it, even though we had to get off the street car at midnight in the worst section of the city and walk down the wharf. Here wharf rats nearly as big as opossums scuttled across our path in the moonlight. But it was quite safe. There was very little crime recorded in the city then. We felt no timidity about walking alone at midnight on poorly lighted streets.[7]

PAY RATE

During World War I, women in the US Navy and Marines received the same pay rate as their male counterparts of the same rank. Their pay started at $28.75 per month, plus $1.25 per day for food and expenses, as well as an allowance for uniforms and medical care. But women's uniforms cost more than those of the men. Women were expected to cover the difference in cost themselves out of their salary.

Some new recruits found themselves doing jobs more complex than boring office work, filling roles such as librarians, fingerprint experts, torpedo assemblers, and switchboard operators.

UNIFORMS

At first, women did not have appropriate uniforms to wear. Men's uniforms would not work for women. Daniels, the secretary of the Navy, remembered decisions about women's uniforms were difficult. He said:

> *Some people thought they ought to wear something like pants. Some had different ideas. The length of the skirt, that was a serious problem. Should we have a long skirt that would sweep the decks? Or something that revealed more leg? Never in my life have I attempted anything, great or small, without the wise counsel of the women. We decided on [skirts] about eight inches from the ground.*[8]

There were also summer and winter-weight hats, boots, leather gloves, and blouses.

It didn't take long for the navy to realize the popularity of women in military dress—patriotism increased wherever they went. During the summer of 1917, the navy sent uniformed women to make appearances at recruiting campaigns, parades, and other official events.

Women filled important clerical positions left vacant as men went to join the fighting.

The inclusion of women in the military in 1917 was a turning point for women's rights. It was a significant occurrence for women and the war. In fact, it would have been impossible for the war to be won without women holding up the structure of the military behind the scenes.

WHAT TO WEAR

Uniforms for enlisted women were a continued source of debate. One newspaper reported on the new recruits' wardrobes:

Pity the navy's poor "yeogirls." They have to have two wardrobes in these days of the high cost of clothes. One [wardrobe] is a thing of strictly tailored garments, made according to Navy specifications and varying not so much as hair's breadth. Government uniforms and their accompaniments have to be of good materials. One cannot scrimp in the amount of material used, or save on its cost. An average, serviceable yeowoman's suit [Norfolk jacket and skirt] costs $35 today. The winter outer garment, which has been specified as the full-length naval cape, lined throughout, is modestly priced at $45.[9]

The whole uniform—suit, plus cape—would cost approximately $1,500 today. Part of the expense would have been covered by their allowance, but it would still have cost more than a month's salary to purchase a uniform.

In the early 1900s, a woman's role in society was considered secondary to a man's. This changed as women joined the war effort. Their contributions during World War I gained women more independence. By the end of the decade, their undeniable impact had helped support arguments for more women's rights, including suffrage.

The yeoman (F) uniform included a navy jacket with gold buttons, an A-line skirt, and a flat-brimmed felt hat.

The assassination of Archduke Franz Ferdinand, *second from left*, triggered the events leading to World War I.

CHAPTER 2

WAR BREAKS OUT

The world changed forever in the summer of 1914. In Sarajevo, Bosnia, a Serbian assassin killed Archduke Franz Ferdinand of Austria-Hungary. The assassin was connected to a pro-Serbian nationalist group called the Black Hand, so Austria-Hungary declared war on neighboring Serbia. Soon, both countries' allies joined the fight.

The main conflict occurred between the Allies and the Central powers. The Allies, led by the United Kingdom, France, and Russia, came to the aid of Serbia. The Central powers were made up of Austria-Hungary and Germany. Before long, more European countries entered the dispute and took sides.

WOMEN FOR PEACE

Unlike other countries, the United States did not immediately enter World War I. President Woodrow Wilson said the United States would stick with its policy of isolationism, which meant it would remain out of the political affairs of other countries. Many US citizens and politicians supported this policy. For a time, the United States sent aid to both sides of the conflict.

In 1915, before the United States entered the war, more and more women became involved in the peace movement. Jeannette Rankin, the first woman

WOODROW WILSON

Woodrow Wilson is sometimes considered one of the first modern presidents. His presidency also marked significant social and cultural changes, including the passage of the Nineteenth Amendment in 1920, which granted women the right to vote.

Wilson was born in Virginia in 1856. His father was a minister, and, after the American Civil War (1861–1865), he served as a professor in South Carolina, during the Reconstruction Era (1863–1877). Through his father, Wilson knew the devastation of war.

Wilson became president of Princeton University in 1902. He then served as the governor of New Jersey before running for president in 1912. Wilson was elected in 1913 and served two terms until 1921. Wilson's most important contribution to the United States was his leadership both during World War I and during the establishment of peace at the war's end. He traveled to Paris, France, to present his proposal for maintaining peace when the Germans signed the armistice. He was the first US president to travel overseas in an official capacity. Wilson suffered a stroke in 1919 that left him paralyzed for the remainder of his presidency. He died on February 3, 1924, in Washington, DC.

JEANNETTE RANKIN

1880–1973

Jeanette Rankin was born on June 11, 1880, in Missoula, Montana. Her parents were a rancher and a schoolteacher. After several careers, including seamstress, social worker, and teacher, Rankin began crusading for women's suffrage.

Women were granted the right to vote in Rankin's home state of Montana in 1914. In 1916, Rankin became the first woman to be elected to serve in the House of Representatives.

After winning the election to the House, Rankin worked tirelessly for peace and the rights of women working in the war effort. A lifelong pacifist, Rankin voted against the resolution approving the United States entrance into World War I. After her term ended in 1919, she continued to focus on peace and women's rights, serving as a delegate to the International Congress of Women.

Rankin returned to the House of Representatives in 1940, elected in part for her stance on peace. She never wavered on her position—she cast the only vote for the United States to remain out of World War II. She

to serve in the House of Representatives, was a lifelong pacifist. Many women joined the American Union Against Militarism (AUAM), which also included male supporters. Peace activists Jane Addams and Carrie Chapman Catt created an organization called the Women's Peace Party (WPP). The leaders of this group consisted of 88 American women.[1]

In April 1915, the WPP participated in the first International Congress of Women, held in the Netherlands, to discuss the idea of peace. More than 2,000 women from warring nations attended, including 47 American women.[2] The US delegates were an elite group who represented education, journalism, social reform, and politics. They knew they had a slim chance of affecting change, but they felt they needed to make a statement. During the four days of conference discussions, women from both the Allied countries and the Central powers came together to discuss ways to put an end to war.

The result of the women's congress was a list of principles required for peace. The list included a requirement that an outside party handle future disputes between nations. It also emphasized the idea that women be granted equal political rights.

When the United States entered the war in 1917, many peace groups splintered over whether to join or remain opposed to the war effort. Addams and other pacifists were considered traitors to the country because they did not support the war. Addams remained true to her cause and helped the

Delegates traveled to the International Congress of Women aboard the MS Noordam.

AUAM develop into the American Civil Liberties Union (ACLU), a nongendered organization founded in 1920 that continues to advocate for individual rights and freedoms today.

Before the United States entered the war, most American loyalties were divided between the Central powers and the Allies. But by 1915, Germany had launched a successful campaign with its U-boats, named for the German word for submarine, *Unterseeboot*. These German submarines sank several cargo ships, including the *Lusitania*, which was a civilian UK ocean liner. It was hit on May 7, 1915, and sank within 20 minutes. Of its 1,959 passengers, 1,198 drowned, including 128 US citizens.[3] Following the incident, American support shifted toward the Allies.

THE UNITED STATES DECLARES WAR

In January 1917, German Secretary of State Arthur Zimmerman sent a coded telegram to Mexican President Venustiano

ATTACKS AT SEA

Between February 1, 1917, and March 18, 1917, German submarines sank six US ships. All crew members managed to escape in lifeboats, until the SS *Vigilancia* sank on March 16. The *Vigilancia* was carrying fruit, iron, and straw, which were considered general cargo. It sailed with a large US flag painted on her side, which could be seen from miles away.

During the escape from the sinking ship, one of the lifeboats was swamped and five US citizens drowned. In the following weeks, two more ships were sunk, the *City of Memphis* and the *Illinois*. All three were announced the same day, causing people to start demanding action from the US government.

Carranza. At the time, Mexico had a strained relationship with the United States. The message proposed that if the United States went to war and opposed Germany, Mexico should ally with Germany in order to regain Texas, New Mexico, and Arizona. British intelligence intercepted the message and relayed it to President Wilson in February 1917. It was later published in the US press. Many Americans began to demand war against Germany.

In March 1917, four US ships were sunk in the German-designated war zone around the United Kingdom. No lives were lost, but these attacks left little doubt that the United States was being deliberately targeted. Finally, on April 6, 1917, the United States declared war on Germany and aligned with the Allies.

When the United States first entered the war, there weren't enough men enrolled in the armed services to go overseas and fight. Unlike the other Allied countries, the United States had not prepared for war, primarily due to its position of isolationism toward conflicts in other parts of the world. At the time, there were approximately 128,000 men in the military.[4] Many of those men served in office positions, helping to keep the military organized and running smoothly. In order to have a viable military capable of fighting, the United States needed to increase its numbers quickly.

MEN LEAVE FOR WAR

To increase the numbers of men in the military, the US government introduced a mandatory draft in May 1917. The draft—called the selective service—legally required all men between the ages of 21 and 30 to register for military service. It was eventually expanded to include men ages 18 to 45. More than 2.8 million men registered for the selective service over the next two years.[5] Even more voluntarily enlisted in the military. As men were called to fight overseas with the Allies, they had no choice but to leave their families and vacate their jobs on the home front. Millions of jobs needed to be filled by capable individuals who could get the work done—both for the military and for nonmilitary needs.

Many Americans initially resisted the widespread hiring of women to fill roles left by departing soldiers. But before the war's end, more than 10 million women had entered the workforce to fill vacated positions and new positions in factories.[6] Soon they were doing work previously designated only for men.

As women said farewell to men, they soon assumed vacant positions that needed to be filled.

Thousands of women gathered at US Marine Corps recruiting stations to enlist as reserves.

WOMEN IN THE ARMED FORCES

The US Navy was the first branch of the armed forces to enlist women to fill the large number of clerical positions left vacant by men sent to fight in the war. Before the war ended in November 1918, approximately 11,000 women had answered the call to join the navy.[1] Though it was the first, the navy was not the only branch to accept female recruits. Other branches such as the US Marine Corps and the US Army followed the navy in enlisting women to serve in various positions during the war.

MARINE CORPS

More than a year after women first enlisted in the navy in 1917, Secretary Josephus Daniels again found himself in a position to approve women for clerical jobs in the military. In August 1918, General George Barnett of the US Marine Corps requested that Daniels approve women to enroll at "corps offices in the United States where their services might be utilized to replace men who may be qualified for active field service."[2]

The Marine Corps began enlisting women as clerks in their Philadelphia office in August 1918. Positions were advertised alongside the slogan "free a man to fight" in the hope that women would fill the clerical positions left vacant by men fighting in the war.[3]

The slogan was effective. After newspapers printed the announcement, thousands of women lined up in front of marine corps offices all over the country.

COAST GUARD

During the outbreak of World War I, the US Coast Guard fell under the authority of the navy. When the navy authorized women to enlist in the naval reserves, the policy was extended to include the coast guard. The mission of the coast guard is to protect the United States' maritime interests and to provide a military presence along the nation's rivers, ports, and ocean borders.

The Coast Guard enlisted a small number of yeomen (F) to serve as volunteers in clerical positions, but personnel records include very few references to these women. Historical records do show, however, that twin sisters Genevieve and Lucille Baker, who transferred from the Naval Coastal Defense Reserve, became the first women to wear coast guard uniforms during World War I.

CHARLOTTE L. WINTERS

While it might seem as though the navy was ahead of the curve on its decision to enlist women, not everyone was in favor of the idea. Newspapers wrote articles against the practice, and people wrote letters expressing their opinions. Many men serving in the military at the time didn't think women belonged. They blamed Secretary Daniels for making a huge mistake.

But it actually might not have been his idea. In 1916, a high school graduate named Charlotte L. Winters requested a meeting with Daniels to ask him why women were not allowed to serve in the navy. Less than a year later, he made his historic decision. Winters enlisted with her sister in 1917. She served as a typist. After the war, she continued to work as a civilian at the Navy Yard in Washington, DC, until she retired in 1953. She later was a member of the American Legion, an organization serving veterans, for 88 years. Winters died in 2007 at age 109, the last female veteran of World War I.[5]

Two thousand women lined up in New York City, New York, after seeing a newspaper article about the marines looking for "intelligent young women."[4]

One of the women who showed up that day was Opha Mae Johnson. At age 18, she had been working as a civilian at Marine Corps Headquarters when the call for enlistees went out. By the war's end, she was promoted to the rank of sergeant.

Jobs for female marines consisted mostly of office work, but they also took part in parades and drills as their navy counterparts did. Reservist Edith Macias said,

Opha Mae Johnson was the first woman to enlist in the US Marine Corps.

At first the male drill instructors were indignant to have been selected to teach drill to women. As a result they showed us no mercy and taught us the same way as they did male recruits.[6]

US ARMY NURSE CORPS

Women in the US Army were limited to serving as nurses. Rather than filling clerical positions as their female counterparts in the navy and the marines did, women in the army were members of the Army Nurse Corps. In April 1917, even before the first troops were deployed, the army nurses were sent to Europe to set up six hospitals.

During the Spanish-American War of 1898, the US Army had hired female nurses on contract. Efforts to hire men to care for the sick had failed, and a typhoid epidemic made it necessary for the army to bring on more than 1,500 female nurses.[7] Many of these nurses stayed on active duty after the Spanish-American War to care for afflicted soldiers, but they did not have military rank or status.

These types of emergency experiences finally resulted in the army and navy creating an official corps of nurses.

Advertisements encouraged women to sign up to be trained as nurses during the war.

In 1901, Congress passed a bill to create a permanent US Army Nurse Corps. This meant a certain number of nurses were kept on reserve status for whenever they were needed. Members of the reserve corps were required to tell the surgeon general where they were living every six months and if they were still able to serve.

In June 1918, toward the war's end, more than 12,000 US Army nurses were on active duty. Almost half of them were overseas. The Army Reorganization Act of 1918 created the Army Nurse Corps and raised members' monthly salary to $60, but it also restricted the type of appointments they could receive. Nurses were not given equal status to male counterparts in both rank or responsibility, and there were certain roles women were not permitted to fill. Their salary was about half of that of male soldiers with an equivalent rank.

To generate a positive response to the war among the public, the US military's wartime propaganda included posters of smiling soldiers and positive slogans. To the large segment of the American public that supported isolationism, the posters helped sell the war. The posters encouraged citizens to participate in the war effort. Some showed pretty young nurses tending to injured soldiers, while others played on the patriotism of Americans. Many Americans, including women, were attracted to enlist as volunteers, nurses, or in the armed forces.

The American Red Cross was integral in recruiting and training qualified nurses for army service. It had maintained a register of qualified nurses for years. Jane A. Delano had been both the chairman of the Red Cross Nursing Service Committee and a second superintendent of the Army Nurse Corps. Delano went to extensive efforts to improve the training of nurses and to standardize the necessary qualifications. The army recognized these efforts, and the Red Cross became the primary supplier of qualified nurses serving in the army. While no nurses were killed fighting in the war, an influenza epidemic of 1918 killed 200 army and 25 navy nurses serving overseas.[8]

INFLUENZA EPIDEMIC OF 1918

An influenza epidemic ravaged the world in 1918. It is estimated 50 million people died that year as a result of the flu, more than one-fifth of the world's population. In the United States, the flu affected 25 percent of the population. In total, it killed more than three times the number of people as World War I itself, which claimed approximately 16 million lives.[10]

ARMY SIGNAL CORPS

A call went out in November 1917 to recruit 100 telephone operators who had the ability to speak French fluently. General John J. Pershing planned to improve communication on the war's western front, turning over US Army switchboards in France to American women. The army had more than 7,500 applicants for the jobs, but many did not have the required ability to speak French. Eventually 150 were sworn in to the United States Army Signal Corps, which managed communications for the armed forces. The first 150 were sent to France for further training, and 450 more were placed on reserve in case they were needed.[9]

Hello Girls helped improve US Army communication by operating the switchboards during the war in France.

These women were known as the Hello Girls. Unlike women serving in the navy and the marines, the Hello Girls who served in the Army Signal Corps did not have official rank. They were paid the same as male soldiers for similarly skilled jobs, but they did not retain veteran status after the war, so they did not receive benefits or postwar services. The 223 women who ultimately filled these roles served in a war zone. They didn't realize they would not be eligible for military status, including medals or honors. If they were injured or captured, they would not have any support from the US military.

Regardless, many of these women wanted to be as close to the action as possible. One recruit, Adele Hoppock, described life as a Hello Girl:

> The girls work only eight hours or less and are taken to the office every day in a Winton Six (automobile). The girls make friends with the officers and they have dances and all sorts of good times. Certain rules, however, must be kept. They cannot be out after dark without a pass, and then there must always be two girls together, "with or without male escort." One rule is quite foolish, I think. They cannot associate with privates or civilians. . . . If I stayed here, I am afraid I would have too good a time. I didn't enlist to be treated like a queen. I expected to rough it and be really in things. I never want to forget the fact that I am here to work hard. We are so proud to be in the service and we feel as though it is a privilege, not our duty, to do our utmost.[11]

Military status was finally granted to the women who served in the Army Signal Corps in 1979, but by then only 18 of them were alive to enjoy the victory.

ARMY NURSES IN EUROPE

The British Expeditionary Force requested medical assistance from the United States in April 1917. In response, the US Army sent medical personnel to Europe, including 200 nurses. The War Department worked with the Red Cross to mobilize people, equipment, and supplies for shipment to France. These were the first organized forces of the United States' involvement in World War I.

The nurses, along with 200 medical officers, were dispatched for service under the British army during the summer of 1917. Their mission was to take over the operation of six base hospitals near the front line. Each of the hospitals had already been operating for three years and serviced approximately 1,000 patients at a time—sometimes more. The British nursing staff stayed to assist with the transition.

The hospital staff was so close to the fighting they were occasionally called to assist with clearing casualties from the front. The nurses treated a constant flow of wounded soldiers. Mary Noble, a nurse from Indiana, remembered,

We dressed their wounds and sent them off by ambulance to the hospital ship—and still they came. We were told that the German army was now within a comparatively few miles. Thirty thousand wounded came through Rouen in ten days and every man received treatment.[12]

Army nurses Edith Ayres and Helen Wood were the first American women to be killed while serving in the War. On May 20, 1917, Ayres and Wood were with Base Hospital No. 12, traveling to France aboard the USS *Mongolia*. During a practice drill, one of the deck guns exploded after the crew fired it. Shell fragments blasted across the deck, killing Ayres and Wood.

After the war ended, women in the navy and the marines were discharged from service. Secretary Daniels said, "As we embrace you in uniform today, we will embrace you without uniform tomorrow."[13]

American Red Cross workers fill a flag with contributions to the war effort.

CIVILIAN WOMEN

Although World War I marked the first time women were officially allowed into military service, women had been active participants in war for years. Women previously contributed to war efforts not with an official rank, but as civilians. During the American Civil War, women served in roles such as spy, soldier, cook, laundress, and scout. Approximately 400 women disguised themselves as men and fought during the war.[1] Approximately 3,000 nurses were employed during the Civil War on both sides of the conflict.[2]

As early as 1914, three years before the United States entered World War I, American women were helping in wartime activities and even heading into war zones as volunteers. More than 25,000 women volunteered overseas during World War I in organizations such as the American Red Cross, the Young Men's Christian

Association (YMCA), the Young Women's Christian Association (YWCA), and the Salvation Army. Many of these volunteers served in nursing roles. But qualified women filled other jobs as well, including doctors, dentists, telephone operators, translators, librarians, architects, journalists, factory workers, drivers, secretaries, and entertainers. They served in aid organizations all over Europe, including the United Kingdom, France, Belgium, Germany, and Italy, as well as Russia and Asia.

A few brave women took the initiative and volunteered wherever they were needed doing whatever was required. Emily Simmonds was on vacation in Paris, in 1914 when the war began. A desperate call for nurses came from war-torn Serbia. At age 26, Simmonds made her way to Serbia. Simmonds employed her nursing background and spent the rest of the war as a Red Cross nurse, volunteering in extreme war conditions. She performed surgery when needed, cooked meals if required, and accompanied escaping civilians out of Serbia.

Many women faced opposition from men who felt women should not be close to the fighting. But for the most part, families were proud of their daughters, and US society approved of women who answered the call to volunteer.

At the start of World War I, the US military didn't have the ability to provide services to boost the morale and social welfare of its soldiers. There were no recreational activities or places for soldiers to socialize. In 1917, US General Pershing, the commander-in-chief of the American Expeditionary Forces, decided

WHY VOLUNTEER?

Ruth Holden, a Red Cross volunteer in World War I, once said, "It isn't exactly an alluring prospect to be exiled in the back woods of Russia for a couple of months with only two English speaking people, to run an infectious hospital, but it will be rather fun."[3]

Women who jumped at the chance to volunteer in the war had to be adventurous and were often looking for a change of life or had a deep sense of patriotism. Most were middle- or upper-class women who could afford to travel. Some had a sincere sense of service or need to help others. Many of them had very little training, but traveled more than 3,000 miles (4,800 km) away, often with no plan for what they were going to do once they got there. In many situations, they found their own work and pitched in where they were needed. Volunteers continued to arrive even after the war's end in February 1918, leading the US State Department to implore would-be volunteers to stay home.

to combine several welfare organizations. The American Red Cross, the YMCA, the YWCA, and the Salvation Army were placed under military supervision.

This restructuring gave each organization specific roles to make it easier to coordinate work, and the government could deploy volunteers as needed through each individual organization. The Red Cross was tasked with caring for the wounded, the YMCA with entertainment and the moral welfare of the soldiers, and the YWCA with providing services to female volunteers and nurses. The Salvation Army provided soldiers with entertainment, Bible study, and home cooking.

AMERICAN RED CROSS

The Red Cross was founded in 1862 by Swiss businessman Henry Dunant as a neutral humanitarian organization that could quickly mobilize during war to care for sick and wounded victims. In 1881, United States nurse Clara Barton founded the American Association of the Red Cross. The mission of the American Red Cross was,

> To furnish volunteer aid to the sick and wounded of the Armed Forces in time of war, and to act in matters of voluntary relief and in accord with military authorities as a medium of communication between the people of the United States and their Armed Forces.[4]

The Red Cross also provided relief to victims of fires, floods, and other natural disasters.

At the beginning of World War I in 1914, the American Red Cross was still relatively young. But when the war began, it was well positioned to offer necessary aid to victims of war. The organization mobilized and sent the SS *Red Cross* to Europe with 170 surgeons and nurses who assisted medical relief units, helping wounded soldiers and victims of war.[5]

The Red Cross is primarily remembered for its high-quality nursing services and volunteers who rushed into action. However, the organization expanded to include social services, such as providing huts with reading and writing rooms

American Red Cross workers serve food and beverages at Union Station in Washington, DC.

for soldiers, establishing lines of communication between soldiers and their families, and cultivating gardens. It also mobilized the collection of scrap metal and newspapers from the Junior Red Cross, an organization of US schoolchildren who helped the war effort. By 1918, the Red Cross had 8.1 million volunteer workers. At the end of the war, approximately one-third of the US population had either donated to the Red Cross or was serving as a volunteer.[6]

In 1916, the American Red Cross was tasked with organizing 50 hospital units, which later became US Army and Navy hospitals in France, England, Ireland, and Scotland. By that time, the Red Cross had a pool of trained nurses who could serve at a moment's notice alongside army or navy reserves.

The Red Cross volunteers were in a position to see the horrible conditions and tragic results of warfare. They tended to injured soldiers but also worked in hospitals full of civilians, including children. France, in particular, was hit hard by tuberculosis. Because most doctors were tending to military troops, there were no medical personnel left to care for the sick. The Red Cross cooperated with local specialists to bring aid to communities that desperately needed medical care.

YMCA

The YMCA began in the United Kingdom before coming to the United States in 1851. George Williams founded the YMCA in 1844 after noticing a need for young

YMCA volunteers work in a mobile kitchen in France.

men to gather around a common purpose and escape the dangers of life on the streets. Retired sea captain Thomas Valentine Sullivan started the first chapter in the United States when he similarly observed a need to create a home away from home for sailors.

During the Civil War, YMCA volunteers worked in the North and the South to provide tents, stationery, books, and other personal services for soldiers. At the time, this was often called "welfare" work because it related to the morale of the soldiers and their mental and physical well-being.

When the United States entered World War I, the YMCA was well established as a volunteer organization with the skills to provide services to the military in the war zone as well as on home soil. In 1917, the YMCA welcomed female volunteers for the first time, and it immediately dispatched a small group to assist in France. At first women were confined to cooking and cleaning in the canteens, or kitchens, because these areas were considered safe. Soon their roles expanded to include other types of welfare service, including reading to soldiers, providing amenities such as cards and cigarettes, and, in the words of YMCA pioneer Dr. Marguerite "Daisy" Crockett, endeavoring to "encourage and hearten the private soldier."[7]

YMCA volunteers Hope Butler and Dr. Crockett both volunteered for the French Army's ambulance unit before the United States entered the war. But in 1917, the YMCA assigned Butler and Crockett to build a hut for the first detachment of US troops. Butler and Crockett overhauled a small building and created a canteen, which served lemonade, hot chocolate, and pastries to US forces throughout the winter of 1917 and 1918. The YMCA offered places for troops to relax and enjoy some downtime. Sometimes canteens showed movies, played music, sold cigarettes, or offered a place to play cards. These huts could also serve as churches, gyms, theatres, or cafés depending on the need.

During World War I, the YMCA operated 1,500 canteens in the United States and France and set up 4,000 huts for recreation and religious services.[8] The YMCA maintained a presence in Europe after the war ended to provide services to troops awaiting approval to return home. After the war, it organized recreational activities and counseling for veterans.

YWCA

Although also committed to helping soldiers, the YWCA's primary mission was to meet the needs of military women on US soil and abroad. The YWCA program focused on recreation, education, training in first aid, and counseling—both personal and spiritual. Social activists Mary Jane Kinnaird and Christian Emma Robarts founded the organization in the United Kingdom in 1855. The first YWCA in the United States was formed in 1858 in New York City.

During World War I, the YWCA joined other women's groups and female army members to campaign for a women's corps to be formed in the US military,

SOCIETY WOMEN IN THE WAR

Two high-profile women offered their services to the YMCA during World War I. Edith Roosevelt and Helen Astor both went to France in the summer of 1917 to volunteer with the YMCA. Edith Roosevelt was the wife of Theodore Roosevelt, the twenty-sixth president of the United States. Four of her sons fought in the war. Roosevelt opened the first canteen in Paris, and her staff organized a series of outdoor activities, including baseball, tennis, volleyball, and other sports. They also established indoor activities, such as theater, movies, and religious services, for soldiers while they were on leave from their duties. After helping to run the canteen in Paris, Roosevelt was asked to design uniforms for the women of the YMCA.

Helen Astor was married to hotel magnate Vincent Astor, who backed social reform through his wealth. Mrs. Astor opened the first canteen for sailors in the port of Brest in France. Because they were from well-known families with wealth, both women were able to volunteer their time and resources.

though this wasn't successfully implemented until the formation of the Women's Auxiliary Corps in 1942.

The YWCA provided hostess houses to serve female American volunteers, nurses, and the Army Signal Corps' Hello Girls. These houses provided amenities such as homey curtains, sewing machines, writing desks, pianos, and Victrolas, a type of early record player. YWCA volunteers acted as housemothers and chaperones, and eventually took the role of career counselors to assist with job placement post-war. The YWCA also operated a Paris hotel for women, which boasted steam heat and hot baths, as well as a restaurant, tearoom, and social spaces.

SALVATION ARMY

Evangeline Booth was the head of the US branch of the Salvation Army when the United States entered World War I. Her father, William, was a minister who started the organization in 1865 when he decided to take his religious message out of the church and into the street.

Booth ran the Salvation Army as a military organization, complete with military rank for its members. The Salvation Army made early contributions to the war effort. Starting with a team of volunteers in New York City, Booth began cutting and rolling linen bandages to ship overseas. By December 1914, the Salvation Army had shipped so many bandages it overwhelmed volunteers at collection sites.

When the United States entered the war in 1917, Booth was ready to send her army overseas. She told General Pershing that she desperately wanted to "send [her] army to France."[9] The first volunteer group traveled to Europe in August 1917.

Similar to the YMCA, the Salvation Army set up service center huts near military camps in France to offer assistance to soldiers. The huts provided recreation and meeting rooms, religious services, and social areas where soldiers could read or write letters.

EVANGELINE BOOTH

1865–1950

Evangeline Booth was born on December 25, 1865, in London, England. Her father, William Booth, founded the Salvation Army in 1865 in East London. She grew up working with her parents and siblings, eventually taking a leadership role at the age of 23. Booth took over command of the Salvation Army forces—which included both men and women—in London and the surrounding area. She was nicknamed The White Angel of the Slums because of both her appearance and musical ability.[10]

Booth became the director of the Salvation Army in Canada from 1896 to 1904 before taking over the role in the United States from 1904 to 1934. Under Booth's leadership, the Salvation Army implemented new services for the elderly and established residences for working women and hospitals for single mothers in addition to its efforts during World War I. The Salvation Army also developed its disaster relief services under Booth's supervision as a reaction to the San Francisco earthquake and fire of 1906. Booth developed an efficient method of fund-raising by fostering support from wealthy public figures. Under her leadership, the organization raised more than $16 million.

Booth received a Distinguished Service Medal in 1919 for her service to the war effort. She retired in 1939 after serving for five years as a Salvation Army general—the organization's highest role. She died on July 17, 1950, at the age of 84.

A Salvation Army volunteer writes a letter for a wounded World War I soldier.

Salvation Army volunteers mended uniforms and made homemade pies and donuts for soldiers. They were often affectionately called "Donut Girls."

While volunteering, Salvation Army workers experienced the war's constant threat of danger. One Salvation Army volunteer, Ethel Renton, recalled making a trip to a nearby town for supplies:

> *Succeeded in renting six pianos at $6.00 a month. While signing the contracts, we heard a siren warning the people of another air attack. The people in this town live in constant fear.*[11]

While they provided entertainment and respite for soldiers, Salvation Army volunteers also lived in dangerous and sparse conditions. In *The War Romance of the Salvation Army*, Evangeline Booth and novelist Grace Livingston Hill described the wartime environment:

> *The life was a hard one for the girls. They nearly froze to death during the days, and at nights they usually shivered themselves to sleep, only sleeping when sheer exhaustion overcame them. There were no baths at all. Even soldiers were at times seen weeping with cold and misery.*[12]

Being a volunteer near the front line of the war could be just as dangerous as being a soldier.

DONUT GIRLS OF THE SALVATION ARMY

The donut became a symbol for the Salvation Army during World War I. In 1917, baking fresh pastries in oil on top of the potbellied stove in a Salvation Army kitchen was backbreaking work.

The smell of frying donuts drew a long line of soldiers. The girls could fry between 2,500 and 9,000 per day. Even when they made other fresh pastries, soldiers continued to call the volunteers "Donut Girls." As a result, World War I soldiers are often called "doughboys." The Salvation Army continues to make donuts, which represent the organization's social concern and readiness to help people in need.

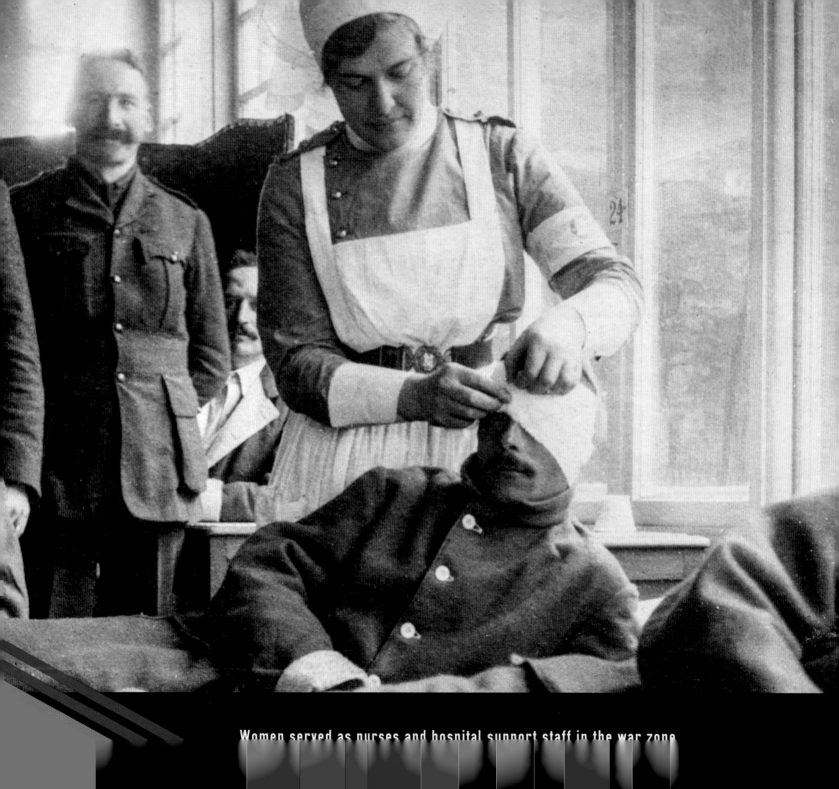

Women served as nurses and hospital support staff in the war zone.

WOMEN SERVING IN THE WAR ZONE

In addition to nurses, the US Army hired female doctors as contract surgeons during World War I, rather than enlisting them and giving them rank. This meant the army didn't have to provide them with military status or pay but could still take advantage of their skill and work ethic. There are no exact numbers of how many female doctors served in World War I. However, the Medical Board of the Council of National Defense (tasked with keeping such records) registered 8,000 women in health-related fields during the war, including doctors, interns, anesthetists, and lab experts.[1] Most of these doctors worked under their own employ—moving from assignment to assignment—wherever they were needed most.

Women also served as support staff for military hospitals all over Europe. Almost all ambulance drivers were women. These women also had the responsibility to fix their ambulances when they broke down. One female doctor wrote,

> While the doctors are in the dispensaries, diagnosing and prescribing, our chauffeurs are under the cars in the wind outside, at the same occupation, and when we see how they make the old, maimed machinery work, we see they are the better MDs.[2]

Drivers were responsible for numerous tasks, including delivering hospital supplies, driving doctors to other facilities, and running errands for the hospitals. Not the least important was ensuring their vehicles were operational and running as smooth as possible for the next duty.

SPIES

Spies worked under dangerous conditions and risked their lives to capture enemy secrets. Both the Allies and Central powers used spies to gather information from the other side in the hopes of finding a weakness to gain an advantage. Women made better spies than men because they were less likely to arouse suspicion.

A large spy network called *La Dame Blanche*, or "The White Lady," employed mostly women to gather information for the Allies from German-occupied Belgium and France. Espionage was a very dangerous occupation, and a captured spy often faced imprisonment or death by firing squad. One of the most famous World War I spies was Mata Hari, who was executed by a French firing squad for spying for the Germans.

Women who were spies usually held other roles as well. Marthe Cnockaert of Belgium was a nurse for Germany, but also worked as a spy for Belgium. When her father was arrested and the family home burned, Cnockaert volunteered to serve as a nurse for both wounded Germans and Belgians at a German hospital in her village. The Germans awarded her the Iron Cross for her service. Another nurse asked Cnockaert to serve as a spy for British Intelligence. Cnockaert accepted the mission and passed along only

MATA HARI

Dutch dancer Mata Hari is quite possibly the most famous spy of all time. She is certainly the most famous female spy. She is best known for wearing elaborate dancing costumes and having relationships with many powerful men. Born in 1857 as Margaretha Zelle, the dancer was accused of passing French secrets to Germany. There is some doubt that she was guilty of this treachery, but she wasn't able to adequately explain the evidence against her. Hari was executed by a French firing squad on October 15, 1917.

intelligence she overheard in the hospital. Eventually, Cnockaert was discovered and sentenced to death, but her sentence was reduced to life imprisonment because of her Iron Cross honor. Cnockaert was released after two years in jail and received praise from the governments of Belgium, France, and the United Kingdom for her efforts.

Because military personnel and volunteers frequently moved around Europe, it was not uncommon for women to be detained and questioned under suspicion as possible spies. Volunteers for the American Red Cross, who moved often to wherever they were most needed, were repeatedly detained and had their credentials questioned by parties on both sides of the conflict.

LIBRARIANS

Books were in high demand from soldiers and volunteers alike—reading was one of the few activities wounded soldiers could enjoy. Books also helped boost morale and provided a connection to home. Both the Red Cross and the Salvation Army

Germans honored Marthe Cnockaert for her nursing while she passed along intelligence to their enemies.

handed out books to those who wanted them. Most huts and canteens housed small libraries.

At the time, most librarians in the United States were women, but male librarians maintained the majority of military libraries. Dr. Herbert Putnam, Librarian of Congress and general director of the American Library Association (ALA) War Service Committee, was adamant that military library work was too difficult for women because it required strength and endurance to pick up and carry heavy boxes of books. Female librarians all over the United States were outraged and vowed to fight against being excluded from military libraries.

Seven women spoke out at the 1918 annual meeting of the ALA to inquire what roles they would be allowed to fill. As a result, women began leaving library employment in order to join the Red Cross and other service groups that employed librarians for the distribution of books from their own organizations.

Along with the protests from women, the ALA also clashed with the Red Cross and the YMCA for control of book distribution. Because of these two major obstacles, the ALA took too much time to get organized, and very few of its librarians were sent to Europe before the war ended. That didn't mean the books didn't get there, though. A number of women made a difference despite opposition from ALA leaders.

Alida M. Stephens of the Library of Congress cataloged the full collection of the ALA war library headquarters in Paris. She created bookcases out of packing

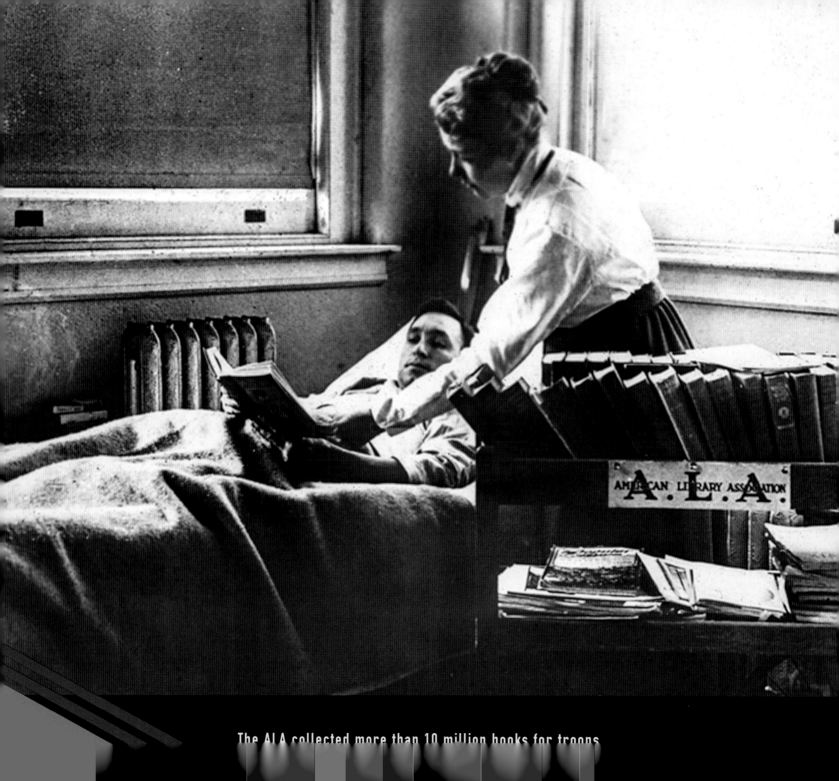

The ALA collected more than 10 million books for troops.

cases and seats out of boards balanced on boxes. Mary Frances Isom, a librarian from Oregon, decided her organizational talents were also needed in Europe. Even though she was in poor health, she spent six months volunteering to organize hospital libraries abroad. She added thousands of books and instituted operational systems for each library. She also offered advice to the workers who were ultimately responsible for managing these libraries. Isom died shortly after she returned from her six months in Europe. Despite its organizational challenges, the ALA collected more than 10 million books for distribution to soldiers.[3]

ENTERTAINERS

During World War I, the Salvation Army, the YMCA, the YWCA, and several other service organizations catered to the emotional needs of troops as one of their core missions. The organizations often overlapped when it came to entertainment and recreational experiences for US troops.

Many women were among the storytellers, actors, and dancers who traveled overseas to entertain the troops during World War I. The YMCA coordinated most of their actions, which was not an easy task. A. M. Beatty, director of the YMCA in Paris, said,

> [F]ortunately we had two 'Y' girls who could [keep track of the entertainers], and these women handled all our actors' expenses with a finesse that

was another modern miracle. They conserved the funds and yet hurt no one's feelings, which was a delicate task. Another 'Y' girl ran our complex card-indexing system, by means of which we knew the movements of every unit and the records and affairs of every individual actor.[4]

Elsie Janis, an American entertainer, was one of the biggest stars to entertain troops during World War I. Starting in 1914, she performed a one-woman show for British and French troops, telling stories and doing imitations. Janis cartwheeled and danced across the stage, much to the delight of the soldiers who responded to her show with applause and cheers.

Sometimes shows were performed in unusual locations, such as churches, train cars, or even the middle of a road or the deck of a ship. Janis often performed her shows in boxing rings. She said of one show,

[The boxing ring] had an enormous crowd on all four sides, which made it rather difficult. I asked them to please close in on three sides, for though I knew the back was the best part of a goose, I was rather scared of an attack from the rear![5]

The YMCA often scheduled performers together for shows. One show might include a singer, someone to accompany the singer on an instrument, and a third person to tell stories or recite poetry. Another group might include a quartet of

Elsie Janis became known as "the sweetheart of the American Expeditionary Force."

choir singers who would lead the crowd in a sing-along as well as singing hymns, opera, and popular songs of the day.

Because entertainers moved around as much, if not more, than the volunteers, they were occasionally suspected of spy activity. Janis was stopped with her mother on their way back to Paris. The French did not understand why two women traveling alone would want to move toward the danger at the front. Entertainers Eunice Prosser Crain and Ruth Bush got lost in the French countryside. The two were arrested on suspicion of being German spies but were able to convince the officials they were not a threat.

Seeing the horrors of war up close wasn't easy for entertainers who performed for the enjoyment of the troops. Singer Mary Rochester Roderick described her experience:

> It has been a hard day for me to sing today, realizing that many of these boys will be killed before this time tomorrow. Tears would come and the only way I managed to sing was to look over their heads and not into their faces. The hard life of trench warfare will leave an effect on our men which they will never lose. How futile it seems. If only I knew just the helpful things to say (or sing) to give them courage. I have felt so inadequate.[6]

Women were often stopped by soldiers while traveling in the war zone.

JOURNALISTS

Americans back home were desperate for news from the front lines. Reporters, both men and women, risked their lives to get close to the action and report back on what they saw. But the various governments involved in the war didn't really want people reporting on their activities. It wasn't unusual for a writer to be arrested as a spy, asked to leave a country, or even fired for doing his or her job. But those threats didn't stop most of them from trying to get the information their readers wanted.

Journalists generally annoyed military leaders, but female journalists particularly did. After all, the leaders reasoned, women did not belong near the war. As a result, it was difficult for women to get credentials that granted them access to military briefings and frontline locations from which they wanted to report. One British reporter, Dorothy Lawrence, posed as a man and became a soldier to access the front lines during the war.

Even so, a number of women traveled to Europe at their own expense to report for newspapers such as the *Chicago Tribune* and the *El Paso Times*. Even with an official news outlet as a sponsor, it was difficult to get to the front lines through traditional means. Some women persuaded local contacts to help them get closer to the action. Others signed up for organizations such as the Red Cross to make their way to the action.

A number of female journalists eventually gave up their quest to report from the front and took on nursing or volunteer positions instead. Reporter Ellen LaMotte volunteered as a nurse after repeatedly being denied access to the front lines. She kept a diary detailing the daily horrors of war. LaMotte turned her diaries into *The Backwash of War*, one of the most popular firsthand accounts

DOROTHY LAWRENCE

Born October 4, 1896, Dorothy Lawrence was determined to become a reporter but faced great opposition from her editors when attempting to access the front lines. "I'll see what an ordinary English girl can accomplish," she said. "I'll see whether I can go one better than these big men with their cars, credentials and money . . . I'll be hanged if I don't try."[7] During the summer of 1915, Lawrence disguised her appearance and became a British soldier. She cut off her brown hair and used a homemade corset stuffed with cotton wool to disguise her figure. Then she convinced two British soldiers to teach her to walk like a man. After securing identification, Lawrence made her way to Amiens, France.

Riding a bicycle, she joined the 179 Tunnelling Company, Fifty-First Division of Royal Engineers in the Somme region of France. The other soldiers helped keep her identity a secret. After almost two weeks in the trenches of the Somme, contaminated water and exhaustion forced Lawrence to reveal her identity to her superiors. Despite having the scoop of a lifetime, the British War Office forbid Lawrence from telling her story publicly until after the armistice in 1918. By the time her book, *Sapper Dorothy Lawrence, The Only English Woman Soldier*, was published in 1919, the world was war-weary. Eventually, Lawrence was committed to an asylum, where she died in 1964.

of the war from the perspective of a nurse in a hospital. The book contained 13 short stories and was first printed in 1916. But due to its harsh depictions of war, which were considered harmful to the morale of the country, the US government halted printing of the book in 1918. It was eventually republished in 1934.

WOMEN AT HOME

The millions of women who didn't enlist in the military or volunteer overseas took care of work and families at home. Many women filled vacancies left by civilian men in factories and other places of employment rather than taking roles with the military. Still others rallied their voices around the call for peace or contributed to the war effort in other ways.

WOMEN IN THE WORKFORCE

The early 1900s saw the continuation of the Industrial Revolution, an age of unprecedented manufacturing that began in the early 1800s. Prior to World War I, women working in factories were mostly young and unmarried. Many were immigrants whose first language was not English, and most jobs for women were in textile

IMMIGRANT FACTORY WORKERS

Twenty-seven million people immigrated to the United States between 1865 and 1916.[1] Very few spoke English, and even fewer had the skills necessary for the jobs available to them. Working in fields in the Southwest or in factories in the Northeast were two of the few options.

Immigrants filled the factories that produced goods for the upper and middle classes of the United States. In large cities, native-born girls joined their immigrant sisters to help their own families. At the start of the 1900s, more than half of the five million women who worked in these industries were under the age of 25.[2]

factories. While men had opportunities to work with skilled tradesmen in apprenticeships, occupations for women consisted of little or no training. The trades filled by women required working rapidly for many hours a day, doing one small piece of a larger task.

The work was repetitive, boring, and dangerous, but for most girls, making a few dollars a week helped their families put food on the table. Factories were full of rows of young women, mostly under the age of 25, doing the same thing. Women in these monotonous jobs considered marriage and children to be the only things that would save them from factory work.

World War I demanded large quantities of ammunition. The US government needed to increase production. The high demand for work in munitions factories resulted in unskilled workers—women and children—working long hours in dangerous conditions to make low wages. Some worked ten-hour shifts for just a few dollars a week.

In 1916, the number of women in government-controlled factories in the United States increased by almost 300 percent.[3] Women made and filled shells and cartridges for weapons and performed other tasks that didn't require any training. These were dangerous jobs, sometimes resulting in death from toxic poisoning or accidental explosions. Yet women sought out the more dangerous munitions jobs because they paid better. Many also found it satisfying to help the war effort.

Factories were dangerous places even if they didn't produce ammunition. Social reformers organized strikes so workers could demand safer working conditions, a limit to the number of work hours, and required rest breaks.

Though there was some resistance to hiring women for what many considered "men's" work, there were few able-bodied men left to hire. Because the jobs needed to get done, women were hired for these open positions both in Europe and in the United States. Munitions factories were the largest employers of women in the United Kingdom in 1918.[4] Other jobs that were traditionally reserved for men, such as ticket collectors, bus drivers, bank tellers, and firefighters, also began hiring women to fill vacancies. These new hires generally received lower pay for the same job. Almost immediately, there were demands for equal treatment.

A woman welds a water jacket, a device which prevents a machine gun from

A little more than five million women were in the UK workforce before the end of the war, repairing rail tracks, working as conductors, delivering mail, and handling baggage.[5] These numbers declined upon the conclusion of the war.

Throughout the war, as men were called to serve their country, women had to do more with less without the traditional money earners of the family. Some middle-class women took in laundry or sewing to make enough money to feed their children. Families in the United States were encouraged to ration their food intake during the war and conserve wheat and other foods. The US Food Administration called the campaign "Food Will Win the War," hoping to feed the US Army and relieve food shortages in Europe. The Food Administration also encouraged rationing specific types of food and supplies, even though it wasn't required.

FARMERETTES

In the early 1900s, approximately half of the US population lived on farms.[6] Agriculture was a major part of the economy, in part because of an increased demand from Europe and the US armed forces. Many of the men who worked the farms were drafted, making it increasingly difficult for farms to meet the demand.

Inspired by a similar program in the United Kingdom, the Women's Land Army of America recruited women from cities to work on farms during World

War I. Between 1917 and 1921, approximately 20,000 young, college-educated women responded.[7] Called "farmerettes," these women agreed to a demanding work ethic that including living in military-style barracks, eating rations without complaint, and living by a strict rule of discipline. Idella Purnell remembered arriving in Napa, California, for the first day on the job:

> It was hot in the orchard at Napa. The sun rose higher and higher, and the long ladders grew heavier and heavier. Perspiration started on our foreheads and beaded our lips. The golden peaches were so high—so hard to reach! The peach fuzz and dust on our throats and arms began to irritate the skin, but we did not dare scratch—we knew that would only aggravate the trouble. One who has never had "peach fuzz rash" cannot appreciate the misery of those toiling, dusty, hot-faced girls.[8]

THE SUFFRAGETTES

The women's suffrage movement began in the mid-1800s. Many people believed it was unfair that women were not allowed the right to vote. Women in the United States and the United Kingdom protested the law, arguing that they should have a say in the decisions affecting their nations. In the United States, Alice Paul and the National Woman's Party organized demonstrations to gain national support for a constitutional amendment.

On August 28, 1917, a group of men and women picketed the White House to pressure President Wilson to support a constitutional amendment that would grant women the right to vote. They carried signs that read, "Mr. President, What Will You Do for Woman Suffrage?" and "How Long Must Women Wait for Liberty?"[9] Protesting started in January, but by August the tone of the protesters had become louder and more personal toward the president. Ten women were arrested. As more and more women were doing men's work for the war effort, it became impossible to argue they could not handle the responsibility of voting. On January 9, 1918, President Wilson publicly announced his support for the amendment. After another year of countless protests, the Senate passed the Nineteenth Amendment on June 4, 1919.

THE KNITTERS

College students, women outside of the workforce, and older women could still support the troops and the war effort. In 1917, the Red Cross made a request for anyone who could knit to immediately begin making knitted clothing for the troops, including sweaters, scarves, and socks. Conditions in the trenches at the front line were awful. Soldiers often spent weeks in muddy and cold weather. Socks were especially needed because soldiers' boots wore through the soles very quickly. Keeping soldiers' feet warm and dry became difficult, but it was necessary to the prevention of foot fungus.

ALICE PAUL

1885–1977

Alice Paul was born on January 11, 1885, in Moorestown, New Jersey. After college at Swarthmore, she traveled to the United Kingdom for graduate work. In London, Paul became involved in the women's suffrage movement. She was arrested several times—and learned to use dramatic strategies to gain attention for a cause.

Paul established the National Woman's Party upon her return to the United States. She was determined to make changes in the lives of women, and did so by methods that were unheard of at the time, including the formation of large-scale demonstrations.

One such demonstration included a parade of 5,000 women's suffrage activists the day before President Woodrow Wilson's 1913 inauguration. Hundreds of thousands of people watched the festivities. Men on the parade route harassed the women and verbally and physically attacked them. The parade was front-page news across the country, successfully putting Paul's message into the national spotlight. Paul died in 1977, having spent her life

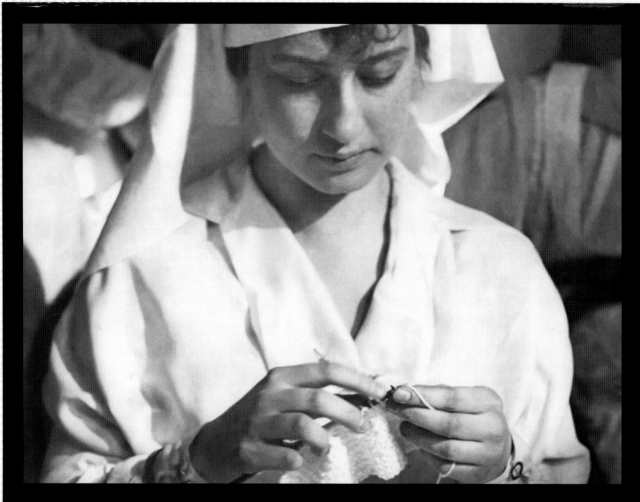

The troops needed a lot of knit clothing, including scarves, sweaters, and socks.

The initial call was for 1.5 million of each type of knitted item, but that number grew.[10] Knitters also produced wool helmets, vests, chest covers, fingerless gloves, and stump socks to cover amputated limbs. The Red Cross coordinated all of the goods and shipped them to the troops. Many women already knew how to knit; men and children learned so they could contribute to the cause.

War propaganda encouraged women to contribute to the war effort by knitting.

AMERICAN RED CROSS

OUR BOYS NEED SOX KNIT YOUR BIT

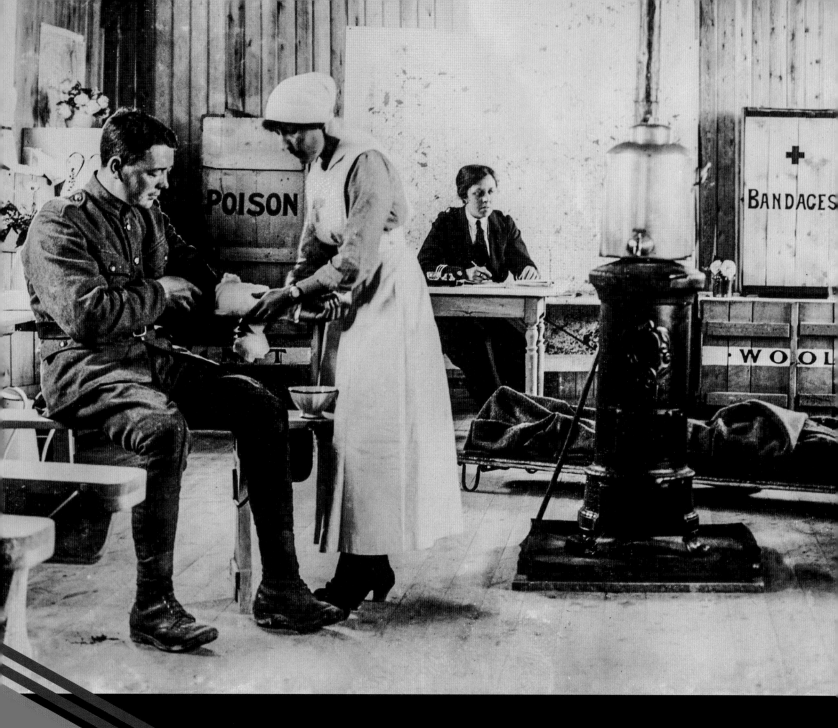

A volunteer assists a soldier at a Voluntary Aid Detachment dressing station.

FOREIGN HEROINES

Women from both Allied and Central powers countries in war-torn Europe routinely risked their lives while participating in the war effort. Because European women were closer to the front lines, their children were closer to the danger as well. Women sacrificed their men—husbands, fathers, friends, and sons—to the fighting. German women had to accept rationing, doing more with less, early on in the war following an Allied blockade of the Central powers.

VOLUNTARY AID DETACHMENT

Women in the United Kingdom mobilized as volunteers soon after the British entered the war in 1914. The British Red Cross organized its volunteers into small groups known as Voluntary Aid Detachments (VAD). More than 90,000 volunteers served in the war, both in the United Kingdom and overseas in France, Italy, and Russia. VADs could be male or female, but because most men were serving in military positions, more than two-thirds of the volunteers were women.[1]

Volunteers had a variety of responsibilities, including nursing, driving, and working at rest stations and auxiliary hospitals. Women were initially trained in first aid, home nursing, and hygiene. If they were tapped as particularly talented, they might learn to use an X-ray machine or study to provide therapeutic massage.

VADs worked under the supervision of nurses, and though their work was less technical, it was equally important. One famous British VAD was mystery novelist Agatha Christie. Christie said the experience was "one of the most rewarding professions that anyone could follow."[2]

After the war began in 1914, the British Red Cross sent nurse Katharine Furse to France with two VADs to set up the

FIRSTHAND ACCOUNT

British VAD Catherine Cathcart-Smith was 24 when she joined the war effort as a VAD in 1914. In 1993 at the age of 104, she gave an interview sharing her experience as a VAD during World War I:

> I wanted to do my bit for the war so I volunteered to drive an ambulance. We had to meet the troop trains at the big London railway stations—Waterloo and Victoria. The trains had hundreds of wounded soldiers packed on them. Their wounds were frightful. Young men with no arms or legs. Many had been gassed. Others blinded. I had two nurses with me, we made a good team. One day I saw this young man on a stretcher. It was my brother, so I said to the soldiers who were carrying him: 'Put him in my ambulance, I am his sister.' When he died the next day I was with him, holding his hand.[3]

first rest station in Boulogne. They provided food and hot drinks and changed bandages for trainloads of soldiers on their way to and from the front line. Furse was later promoted to the position of commander-in-chief and placed in charge of the VAD department in London.

Women were not allowed on the war's front lines at first, but by 1915 military leaders allowed volunteers above the age of 23 and with more than three years of experience to be closer to the fighting. Once at the front, VADs drove ambulances and wrote letters for wounded soldiers.

DISGUISES AND ALL-FEMALE BATTALIONS

Some European women attempted to serve on the front lines in secret. Russian Natalie Tychmini disguised herself for combat. She fought against the Austrians in Opatów, Poland, in 1915 and received the Cross of Saint George for distinguished service. An injury ultimately revealed that she was really a woman. Olga Krasilnikova was another Russian woman who received the Cross of Saint George. Krasilnikova participated in 19 battles in Poland. Like Tychmini, Krasilnikova was discovered when she was wounded and sent home.

At the beginning of the war, Russian military leaders didn't approve of women in the armed forces. But by the time Russia exited the war in 1917, the government had changed tactics. It started when wives and daughters of officers began disguising themselves as men to secretly enlist in the military.

AGATHA CHRISTIE

1890–1976

Agatha Christie was born on September 15, 1890, in Torquay, Devonshire, England. Long before she became a best-selling writer of crime novels, Christie was a nurse in World War I. At 24 years old, she volunteered at her local Red Cross hospital while her husband served in France as a pilot for the British army.

She assisted in surgery, wrote letters for illiterate soldiers, and helped other nurses cope with the horrors of war. She was also assigned to the hospital dispensary, or pharmacy. It was boring compared to nursing, but she learned about a variety of medicines and poisons. While she waited for patients to come, she started thinking about writing a detective story. Christie's first novel, *The Mysterious Affair at Styles*, was published in 1920 and featured Belgian detective Hercule Poirot, one of her most famous characters. Poirot would appear in 33 of Christie's novels. Before her death in 1976, Christie wrote 66 mystery novels and 153 short stories.

As more men were disabled, the Russian government began to consider the idea of allowing women in more dangerous military positions. In fact, there were several all-female battalions, one founded by a Siberian peasant named Maria Bochkareva. Her group, nicknamed The Battalion of Death, was hailed in the British press:

> [Bochkareva] . . . formed a battalion of 260 women, sworn to conquer or die. . . . These women fought behind the famous Siberian Ironsides [nickname of the first Siberian Army], took German prisoners and lost many killed and wounded.[4]

Members of a Russian women's regiment relax at their camp.

ON THE HOME FRONT

Plenty of women who did not volunteer in official capacities or make their way to the front line still supported their countries in vital ways. Women in the United Kingdom, Italy, and France took jobs in factories, and their roles within the factories expanded to include jobs typically held by men.

As German men left to join the fighting, their wives and daughters went to work in order to make up for lost income and fill vacant jobs. But they often only made half the salary men would have made doing the same job. In some cases, women who did not receive equal treatment chose to strike against their government for more balanced treatment. A 1917 strike by women in Russia is considered partially responsible for sparking the Russian Revolution.

In Italy, many women who lived in cities were recruited to the country to farm. They were needed to replace men and draught animals, such as horses, that were taken to the front lines. In many European cities, women and children had no choice but to wait in line to buy rotten potatoes or to scavenge in public parks for trash that might contain a scrap of food.

The British blockade of Germany also prevented the import of goods, which created a shortage of food and other supplies. As food became scarce, children and the elderly began to suffer from malnutrition. German women felt even more

Food shortages
breadlines.

pressure to make enough money to feed their families, as men were not likely to return. By 1918, more than two million women in Germany were widows.[5]

In an appeal to German patriotism, women were asked to cut their long hair to donate to the war effort. Human hair was used to make transmission belts for vehicles. They also consumed ersatz, or substitute, products to aid in conservation of food and supplies. Rather than coffee, German citizens drank a substitute from roasted acorns. *Kriegsbrot*, or war bread, was made of rye, wheat, potato meal, sugar, and shortening. Eventually, alternatives such as oats, corn, beans, and peas were added to the recipe. Despite its combination of substitute ingredients, *kriegsbrot* was considered very edible and a loaf lasted up to a week.

Germany's 1915 naval blockade of the United Kingdom, as well as poor harvests in 1917, threatened the British population with starvation. In response, the United Kingdom's Board of Agriculture responded by establishing the Women's Land

FOOD SHORTAGES AND RATIONING

European countries greatly suffered from food shortages during the war. Farms that weren't turned into battlefields didn't get the necessary fertilizers, which reduced agricultural production and resulted in higher food prices. Some governments responded by putting price controls on foodstuffs. It was common for women and children to stand in food lines throughout Europe. Eventually, in Russia, Turkey, and Austria-Hungary, distribution via food lines resulted in rioting. The British naval blockade forced Germany to introduce controls on food production and sale. But these controls were poorly planned and amplified the effects of the blockade, causing malnourishment among Germans. Many Allied countries later implemented mandatory food rationing on their citizens, including the United Kingdom in 1918.

The Women's Land Army was the United Kingdom's response to food shortages caused by Germany's naval blockade.

Army (WLA). More than 250,000 women volunteered to become so-called Land Girls and fill the farming positions left vacant by men serving in the war.[6] The WLA became vital to the British victory on the home front.

Land Girl Agnes Greatorex recalled waking at 5:00 a.m. to milk cows and taking the milk to the nearby hospital. Then she would plow fields and cut trees, often working alongside prisoners of war. Greatorex said being a Land Girl during World War I made her and other women independent. "I think the First World War did change women. Because once they'd had a taste they wouldn't go back to service, they were free," Greatorex said.[7]

Working as volunteers or in factories, women made many contributions during

8

THE GREAT WAR'S IMPACT ON WOMEN

World War I ended in November 1918 when Germany accepted the terms of armistice from the Allies. In the end, approximately 9 million men were killed and 21 million were wounded.[1]

The war resulted in many changes in attitudes towards society and social behavior. Many people questioned their long-held beliefs about social classes and work. Attitudes toward women and their role in society began to change now that they had played a crucial role in the war effort.

Before World War I, women had not served in the US military in any capacity other than nursing. While military leaders were slow to treat them with equal status to their male counterparts, many women stepped up to the call of duty and served their country. This was a turning point in the women's movement. Twenty years later, when World War II (1939–1945) began, the experiences of women during World War I allowed the expansion of roles and acceptance of women serving in the US military.

CHANGES AND CHALLENGES

After the war ended, the primary goal for all involved was returning to "normal." This meant men came home to resume their positions in factories and farms, while women were expected to return to their roles in the home.

The world expected women to quietly resume their old lives. But for women who had seen independence for the first time, it was difficult to return to being dependent on men. As one female wartime medical worker said,

> *The girls had been able to take care of themselves, to be trusted in unusual and untried positions. The war had helped the advancement of women in comradely endeavor with men. But somehow, somewhere, now that the emergencies no longer existed, the code of good society was broken, the pattern was gone.*[2]

Men who returned from war were encouraged to get back to their lives, even though many were wounded and would never be the way they were before the war. Rehabilitation services were scarce, with very little support to help men live with what they'd experienced while overseas. The best advice the military could give veterans was to get back to their regular lives.

Women were forced to give up their jobs for the men returning from the war.

In most situations, women had no choice but to vacate the positions they'd filled and return to the lives they were expected to lead. Some returned to the home, while others performed what was commonly considered women's work with laundry and textiles. Even widows were fired from jobs to make room for the 50 million men who returned from war between 1918 and 1919.[3]

Some women refused to go back to the way things were, going on to have careers in government and social welfare organizations. Other women took the skills they learned in the war and earned additional degrees and careers. The post-1914 world experienced major changes in politics, technology, and social norms.

Women who served during the war made practical modifications to the accepted fashions of the time. Before the war, women wore long skirts brushing the ground. Women in the war zone often wore pants, especially ambulance drivers who sometimes had to crawl under their cars to make repairs. Many women cut their hair short because it was too hard to keep clean and free of lice. Shorter hemlines and less constricting clothing became more accepted as the 1900s progressed.

After the war, women's roles continued changing—they had more freedom and rights than ever before. The United States became more prosperous, and styles became less conservative. Many women reflected this shift by rejecting

During the war, women started wearing their husbands' pants. They continued to

the old-fashioned looks of earlier decades and embracing shorter skirts and more comfortable clothing.

WOMEN'S SUFFRAGE

While women were allowed to vote in some local and state elections prior to 1920, they were not granted the right to vote in national elections. In 1918, President Woodrow Wilson started to publicly support women's suffrage in the United States, in part because of women's influence during the war. During a speech before Congress, Wilson said,

> *We have made partners of the women in this war . . . Shall we admit them only to a partnership of suffering and sacrifice and toil and not to a partnership of privilege and right?*[4]

In 1920, the Nineteenth Amendment to the US Constitution finally gave women in the United States the right to vote in national elections. More than 8 million women voted in US elections on November 2, 1920.[5]

After the passing of the Nineteenth Amendment, women began to run for political office as well. In 1928, there were seven women in the US House of Representatives and hundreds more serving in state legislatures.[6] Edith Nourse Rogers was elected to the House of Representatives in 1925. Until 2012, Rogers had served in Congress longer than any other woman.

Women in the United States celebrate the Nineteenth Amendment

EDITH NOURSE ROGERS

Edith Nourse Rogers from Lowell, Massachusetts, was a Red Cross volunteer nurse during World War I. In 1925, she became one of the first women to serve in the US Congress when she was elected to the House of Representatives. Rogers ran for the seat of her late husband, John Jacob Rogers, when he died in 1925.

Rogers was instrumental in introducing the Women's Army Auxiliary Corps (WAAC) in 1941 as a voluntary program for women to join the US Army. The WAAC Act gave opportunities to 150,000 women to serve in a variety of positions, including cooks, messengers, postal workers, chauffeurs, and hundreds of other army jobs. Rogers, an advocate for veterans benefits and equality for women, served in the House of Representatives for 35 years until her death in 1960.

Women over the age of 30 in the United Kingdom were given the right to vote in 1918. It took ten more years to lower the voting age. In 1928, the Equal Franchise Act was passed, granting all women in the United Kingdom over the age of 21 the right to vote.

Most governments acknowledged the contribution of women during the war. Soon after fighting ended, women won the right to vote in other countries, including Canada, the German Republic, Austria, Hungary, and Czechoslovakia.

RECOGNITION FOR SERVICE

The US government—which had actively recruited women to serve overseas in World War I—took decades to grant women the same post-war benefits as men.

Women who had sustained injuries as a result of their service were not admitted to veterans' hospitals. Women were not eligible to earn awards or medals of achievement. Eventually, the Army-Navy Nurses Act of 1947 recognized their service. The act presented women who served in World War I with honorable discharges from military services.

It took until 1979 for the Hello Girls to win their fight for recognition as veterans. However, most of the survivors did not harbor hard feelings. Esther Fresnel Goodall, who had served as a Hello Girl in France, said,

> I really felt it was my mission to talk on the telephone. When I was off duty I sometimes spent the whole night talking on the phone with the boys at the Front. I kept thinking it might be their last night.[7]

LEGACY

World War I is often considered to be the first time many American and European women had significant independence from men. Millions of women became the head of households, earned money for their families, and made decisions about what to do without the input of a husband or father.

Women had new privileges and freedoms during World War I they had never experienced before. Many women found it hard to return to being treated as though they were second-class citizens with no status and no say in their own lives. When the fighting in Europe ended, a new battle was beginning at home as

WOMEN IN COMBAT TODAY

Over the decades, women have served in increasingly dangerous roles in the US military. Today, there are more than 200,000 women in the service, making up nearly 14.5 percent of the total active-duty force.[8] Almost 70 are generals or admirals. Until 2013, women were still banned from serving in specialty units such as armor, artillery, and infantry. In response to lifting the ban on women in combat, Defense Secretary Leon Panetta said,

> [Women] have become an integral part of our ability to perform our mission, and for more than a decade of war they have demonstrated courage and skill and patriotism. If members of our military can meet the qualifications for a job—and let me be clear, I'm not talking about reducing the qualifications for the job—if they can meet the qualifications for the job, then they should have the right to serve, regardless of creed or color or gender or sexual orientation.[9]

As of 2015, 29 women attempted to pass the rigorous Marine Corps Infantry Officer's course. None were successful, and frontline combat remained out of reach for women.

women fought to gain equal veterans benefits, keep needed jobs for income, and secure the right to vote.

Things have changed a lot during the last 100 years. Throughout the 1900s, women progressively took on more responsibility in the military. Today, women not only serve alongside male soldiers, but they have been promoted to leadership roles in the military and have commanded troops. There are still areas in which women are excluded, including some combat positions, but great strides have been made. The military service of women during World War I laid a foundation for the future. During World War II, more than 60,000 women served in the military as army nurses and Women Airforce Service Pilots (WASP). The navy, the marines, and the coast guard also enlisted more women, bringing the total to more than 400,000 women serving in the US armed forces during World War II.[10]

Women not only influenced World War I's conclusion, but they also influenced the outcome for themselves as well. As World War I historian Dr. Gerry Oram said,

> *There was little point in pretending anymore—women had proved they could take on any role a man had done, and they'd played an enormous part in winning the war.*[11]

WASPS OF WWII

During World War II, approximately 1,100 civilian women were trained to fly military aircraft in order to release male pilots for combat.[12] Many of them had scrimped together enough money to take flying lessons and get their pilot's license in order to enlist.

The female pilots were called the Women Airforce Service Pilots (WASPs). For two years, between 1942 and 1944, WASPs flew every type of military aircraft, ferrying new planes to military bases and flying targets for shooting practice.

These civilian women weren't granted official military status until the 1970s. In July 2010, President Barack Obama signed a bill awarding the WASPs the Congressional Gold Medal, the highest civilian honor given by the US Congress.

TIMELINE

1914

World War I begins on
July 28.

1914

The American Red Cross
sends 170 surgeons and
nurses to help wounded
soldiers.

1914

Elsie Janis starts
performing a one-woman
show for British and
French troops.

1915

The first International
Congress of Women is
held in the Netherlands in
April.

1917

In November, the US Army
recruits the Hello Girls,
100 telephone operators
to work as translators in
France.

1917

The Salvation Army's
Donut Girls fry between
2,500 and 9,000 donuts
per day for soldiers.

1917

For the first time, the
YMCA welcomes female
volunteers and dispatches
a small group to France.

1918

Opha Mae Johnson
becomes the first woman
to enlist in the US Marine
Corps.

1917

Women are allowed to enlist in the US Navy in March.

1917

The US Army sends medical personnel to Europe, including 200 nurses.

1917

The United States declares war on Germany on April 6.

1917

Women start filling factory jobs after a mandatory draft calls men to military service in May.

1918

The Red Cross has 8.1 million volunteer workers.

1918

World War I ends on November 11.

1919

Evangeline Booth receives a Distinguished Service Medal for her service to the war effort.

1920

The Nineteenth Amendment grants women in the United States the right to vote.

ESSENTIAL FACTS

KEY PLAYERS

- Loretta Perfectus Walsh was the first of 200 women to enlist as yeomen (F) in the US Navy on March 17, 1917.

- Jeannette Rankin was a pacifist and the first woman elected to the House of Representatives in 1916.

- Salvation Army director Evangeline Booth developed a successful method of fund-raising and organized her army of volunteers to help with the war effort.

- Alice Paul established the National Woman's Party, which fought for women's suffrage.

KEY STATISTICS

- Approximately 11,000 women answered the call to join the US Navy during World War I.

- By the end of the war, more than 12,000 US Army nurses were on active duty.

- By 1918, the Red Cross had 8.1 million volunteer workers assisting with the war effort.

- Approximately 20,000 women volunteered as farmerettes in the United States and more than 250,000 women volunteered to become Land Girls in the United Kingdom.

IMPACT ON THE WAR

The various roles women played in the war effort are considered vital to winning the war. Starting with the US Navy in 1917, women were allowed to enlist in the armed forces. These enlistees helped complete clerical and other work left behind when men left to fight in the war. Women ran households and worked in factories, filling vital positions left vacant by men. They helped produce munitions and other supplies for the war effort. Other women raised funds and volunteered with organizations overseas such as the Salvation Army, Red Cross, YMCA, and YWCA. These women nursed injured soldiers, ran canteens, and provided entertainment to boost soldier morale. Because the fighting took men away from farms, the farmerettes in the United States and Land Girls in the United Kingdom helped maintain food supplies.

IMPACT ON SOCIETY

Through their involvement in the war effort, many women experienced independence for the first time during World War I. After the war, women continued to experience new freedoms as their role in society changed. The important work of women at home and in the war zone increased support for a constitutional amendment granting women the right to vote. On August 18, 1920, the US Congress passed the Nineteenth Amendment, which granted suffrage to women. With their service in the military, women paved the way for those serving in World War II and beyond.

QUOTE

"There was little point in pretending anymore—women had proved they could take on any role a man had done, and they'd played an enormous part in winning the war."

—*Dr. Gerry Oram, World War I historian*

GLOSSARY

ARMISTICE
A temporary stop of fighting by mutual agreement.

AUXILIARY
Reserves separate from the regular armed forces and used for assistance during wartime.

CIVILIAN
A person not serving in the armed forces.

DEPLOY
To spread out strategically; to send into battle.

DRAFT
A system in which people of a certain age are required to register for military service.

DRAFTSMAN
Someone who makes drawings of machines or other plans or designs.

ENLIST
To voluntarily join the military.

ESPIONAGE
The practice of spying.

FRONT
An area where a battle is taking place.

MUNITION
War supplies.

NEUTRAL
To not favor either side in a conflict, such as a war.

PROPAGANDA
Information used to support a political group or point of view, or to persuade the audience to support their country's participation in a war.

RATIONING
Setting limits on the amount of certain foods or materials a population can purchase during war or other conflicts.

STENOGRAPHER
A person who can use shorthand to take notes or write letters as someone dictates to them.

SUFFRAGE
The right to vote in a political election.

ADDITIONAL RESOURCES

SELECTED BIBLIOGRAPHY

Brown, Carrie. *Rosie's Mom: Forgotten Women Workers of the First World War*. Boston, MA: Northeastern U, 2002. Print.

Dowling, Timothy C. *Personal Perspectives*. Santa Barbara, CA: ABC-CLIO, 2006. Print.

Schneider, Dorothy, and Carl J. Schneider. *Into the Breach: American Women Overseas in World War I*. New York: Viking, 1991. Print.

FURTHER READINGS

Anderson, Jennifer Joline, and Arzoo Osanloo. *Essential Library of Social Change: Women's Rights Movement*. Minneapolis: Abdo, 2014. Print.

Atwood, Kathryn J. *Women Heroes of World War I: 16 Remarkable Resisters, Soldiers, Spies, and Medics*. Chicago, IL: Chicago Review, 2011. Print.

Pratt, Mary K. *Essential Library of American Wars: World War I*. Minneapolis, MN: Abdo, 2014. Print.

WEBSITES

To learn more about Essential Library of World War I, visit **booklinks.abdopublishing.com**. These links are routinely monitored and updated to provide the most current information available.

PLACES TO VISIT

National Women's History Museum
205 S. Whiting Street Suite 254
Alexandria, VA 22304
703-461-1920
http://www.nwhm.org
The museum offers online exhibits and educational resources on women's history.

National World War I Museum at Liberty Memorial
100 W. Twenty-Sixth Street
Kansas City, MO 64108
816-888-8100
https://theworldwar.org/explore/collections
The museum houses more than 75,000 artifacts telling the story of the Great War from the beginning to the armistice.

World War I Historical Association (WWIHA)
2625 Alcatraz Avenue, #237
Berkeley, CA 94705-2702
http://ww1ha.org/the-first-world-war
The WWIHA offers books, lectures, and annual events to promote interest in the war and preserve the memory of those who served their nations.

SOURCE NOTES

CHAPTER 1. IN THE NAVY

1. "The Price of Freedom: Yeoman (F) Uniform." *Smithsonian*. Smithsonian, n.d. Web. 9 Sept. 2015.

2. Lettie Gavin. *American Women in World War I: They Also Served*. Boulder, CO: U of Colorado, 1997. Print. 2.

3. Ibid. 10.

4. Ibid. 13.

5. Ibid.

6. Ibid. 5.

7. Ibid. 7.

8. Ibid. 4.

9. Ibid.

CHAPTER 2. WAR BREAKS OUT

1. Dorothy Schneider and Carl J. Schneider. *Into the Breach: American Women Overseas in World War I*. New York: Viking, 1991. Print. 248.

2. Ibid. 252.

3. "World War I." *The World Book Encyclopedia*. Chicago, IL: World Book, 2011. Print. 462.

4. Ibid.

5. "Selective Service Acts." *Encyclopaedia Britannica*. Encyclopaedia Britannica, 2015. Web. 9 Sept. 2015.

6. Sheila Rowbotham. *A Century of Women: The History of Women in Britain and the United States in the Twentieth Century*. New York: Penguin, 1999. Print. 104.

CHAPTER 3. WOMEN IN THE ARMED FORCES

1. Evelyn Monahan and Rosemary Neidel-Greenlee. *A Few Good Women*. New York: Knopf, 2010. Print. 8.

2. Lettie Gavin. *American Women in World War I: They Also Served*. Boulder, CO: U of Colorado, 1997. Print. 25.

3. Ibid. 26.

4. Ibid.

5. Joe Holley. "Charlotte Winters, 109; World War I Sailor And U.S. History Buff." *Washington Post*. Washington Post, 30 Mar. 2007. Web. 10 Sept. 2015.

6. Lettie Gavin. *American Women in World War I: They Also Served*. Boulder, CO: U of Colorado, 1997. Print. 31.

7. Dorothy Schneider and Carl J. Schneider. *Into the Breach: American Women Overseas in World War I*. New York: Viking, 1991. Print. 8.

8. "Highlights in the History of the Army Nurse Corps: Chronology." *Highlights in the History of the Army Nurse Corps: Chronology*. US Army Center of Military History, 19 Jan. 2001. Web. 10 Sept. 2015.

9. Evelyn Monahan and Rosemary Neidel-Greenlee. *A Few Good Women*. New York: Knopf, 2010. Print. 10.

10. "The Deadly Virus: The Influenza Epidemic of 1918." *National Archives*. National Archives, n.d. Web. 10 Sept. 2015.

11. Lettie Gavin. *American Women in World War I: They Also Served*. Boulder, CO: U of Colorado, 1997. Kindle.

12. "Women in Service in the Great War." *WorldWar1Vets.com*. WorldWar1Vets.com, n.d. Web. 10 Sept. 2015.

13. "Coast Guard Women's Reserve." *Encyclopaedia Britannica*. Encyclopaedia Britannica, 2015. Web. 10 Sept. 2015.

CHAPTER 4. CIVILIAN WOMEN

1. Dorothy Schneider and Carl J. Schneider. *Into the Breach: American Women Overseas in World War I.* New York: Viking, 1991. Print. 7.

2. "Women in the Civil War." *History.com.* History.com, n.d. Web. 10 Sept. 2015.

3. Dorothy Schneider and Carl J. Schneider. *Into the Breach: American Women Overseas in World War I.* New York: Viking, 1991. Print. 21.

4. Lettie Gavin. *American Women in World War I: They Also Served.* Boulder, CO: U of Colorado, 1997. Print. 179.

5. Evelyn Monahan and Rosemary Neidel-Greenlee. *A Few Good Women.* New York: Knopf, 2010. Print. 13.

6. "World War I and the American Red Cross." *American Red Cross.* American Red Cross, n.d. Web. 10 Sept. 2015.

7. Lettie Gavin. *American Women in World War I: They Also Served.* Boulder, CO: U of Colorado, 1997. Print. 130.

8. "History—1900 to 1950s." *YMCA.* YMCA, 2015. Web. 10 Sept. 2015.

9. Lettie Gavin. *American Women in World War I: They Also Served.* Boulder, CO: U of Colorado, 1997. Print. 209.

10. "Evangeline Cory Booth." *Encyclopaedia Britannica.* Encyclopaedia Britannica, 2015. Web. 10 Sept. 2015.

11. Lettie Gavin. *American Women in World War I: They Also Served.* Boulder, CO: U of Colorado, 1997. Print. 213.

12. Ibid.

CHAPTER 5. WOMEN SERVING IN THE WAR ZONE

1. Dorothy Schneider and Carl J. Schneider. *Into the Breach: American Women Overseas in World War I.* New York: Viking, 1991. Print. 95.

2. Ibid. 98.

3. Linton Weeks. "When America's Librarians Went to War." *NPR.* NPR, 4 July 2015. Web. 10 Sept. 2015.

4. James W. Evans and Gardner L. Harding. *Entertaining the American Army.* New York: Association Press, 1921. Print. 55.

5. Dorothy Schneider and Carl J. Schneider. *Into the Breach: American Women Overseas in World War I.* New York: Viking, 1991. Print. 159.

6. Ibid. 167.

7. Sarah Oliver. "Incredible Story of the Only British Woman to Fight in the Trenches." *Daily Mail.* Daily Mail, 12 Jan. 2014. Web. 10 Sept. 2015.

SOURCE NOTES
CONTINUED

CHAPTER 6. WOMEN AT HOME

1. Laurence Gerckens. "Ten Events That Shaped the 20th Century American City." *PlannersWeb*. PlannersWeb, 1998. Web. 10 Sept. 2015.

2. Carrie Brown. *Rosie's Mom: Forgotten Women Workers of the First World War*. Boston, MA: Northeastern UP, 2002. Print. 8.

3. Susan R. Grayzel. "Women's Mobilization for War." *International Encyclopedia of the First World War*. International Encyclopedia of the First World War, 8 Oct. 2014. Web. 10 Sept. 2015.

4. "World War I: 1914-1918." *Striking Women*. Striking Women, n.d. Web. 10 Sept. 2015.

5. Robert Wilde. "A History of Women and Work in World War 1." *About Education*. About, n.d. Web. 10 Sept. 2015.

6. Carolyn Dimitri, Anne Effland, and Neilson Conklin. "The 20th Century Transformation of U.S. Agriculture and Farm Policy." *USDA*. USDA, June 2005. Web. 10 Sept. 2015.

7. "Woman's Land Army of America, ca WWI." *The Victory Grower*. University of California, 2015. Web. 10 Sept. 2015.

8. Elaine F. Weiss. "Before Rosie the Riveter, Farmerettes Went to Work." *Smithsonian*. Smithsonian, 29 May 2009. Web. 10 Sept. 2015.

9. "Today in History: August 28—Picketing for Suffrage." *Library of Congress*. Library of Congress, 11 Jan. 2011. Web. 10 Sept. 2015.

10. "The Roles of Women in the War." *Skwirk Education*. Skwirk, n.d. Web. 10 Sept. 2015.

CHAPTER 7. FOREIGN HEROINES

1. "Women's Involvement with the British Red Cross During the First World War." *British Red Cross*. British Red Cross, 2015. Web. 10 Sept. 2015.

2. "Volunteers during the First World War." *British Red Cross*. British Red Cross, 2015. Web. 10 Sept. 2015.

3. "Catherine Cathcart-Smith." *Spartacus Educational*. Spartacus Educational, 1997. Web. 10 Sept. 2015.

4. Patrick Wingrove. "Russia's Heroic 'Battalion of Death'" *The Illustrated First World War*. The Illustrated First World War, 13 Aug. 2014. Web. 10 Sept. 2015.

5. "Life on the German Home Front During the First World War." *Centenary News*. Centenary News, 1 Apr. 2013. Web. 10 Sept. 2015.

6. Neil Prior. "How Land Girls Helped Feed Britain to Victory in WW1." *BBC News*. BBC News, 26 Feb. 2014. Web. 10 Sept. 2015.

7. Ibid.

CHAPTER 8. THE GREAT WAR'S IMPACT ON WOMEN

1. "WWI Casualty and Death Tables." *PBS*. PBS, n.d. Web. 10 Sept. 2015.

2. Dorothy Schneider and Carl J. Schneider. *Into the Breach: American Women Overseas in World War I*. New York: Viking, 1991. Print. 278.

3. Belinda Davis. "The Mighty Women of World War I." *CNN*. CNN, 2 July 2014. Web. 10 Sept. 2015.

4. "Woodrow Wilson and the Women's Suffrage Movement: A Reflection." *Global Women's Leadership Initiative*. Wilson Center, 4 June 2013. Web. 10 Sept. 2015.

5. "19th Amendment." *History.com*. A&E, 2010. Web. 10 Sept. 2015.

6. Lynn Dumenil. "The New Woman and the Politics of the 1920s." *Harry S. Truman Library and Museum*. Harry S. Truman Library and Museum, 1 July 2007. Web. 10 Sept. 2015.

7. Lettie Gavin. *American Women in World War I: They Also Served*. Boulder, CO: U of Colorado, 1997. Print. 93.

8. "Women in the Military Statistics." *Statistic Brain*. Statistic Brain, 27 Dec. 2013. Web. 10 Sept. 2015.

9. "Sec. Panetta and Gen. Dempsey's Media Briefing." *Joint Chiefs of Staff*. Joint Chiefs of Staff, 24 Jan. 2013. Web. 10 Sept. 2015.

10. "World War II: Women and the War." *Women in Military Service For America Memorial Foundation*. Women in Military Service For America Memorial Foundation, n.d. Web. 10 Sept. 2015.

11. Neil Prior. "How Land Girls Helped Feed Britain to Victory in WW1." *BBC News*. BBC News, 26 Feb. 2014. Web. 10 Sept. 2015.

12. "WASP: Women With Wings In WWII." *NPR*. NPR, 9 Mar. 2010. Web. 10 Sept. 2015.

INDEX

ABOUT THE AUTHOR

Kristine Carlson Asselin is the author of more than a dozen children's books for the elementary school and library market. In addition to nonfiction, she writes young-adult and middle-grade fiction. She has a BS from Fitchburg State University and an MA from the University of Connecticut. She lives with her husband and daughter in a suburb of Boston, Massachusetts.